THE ART OF GROWING DAHLIAS

Tips and tricks for first-time gardeners

A Y de Vink

To the dahlia man himself, my brother-in-law, Paul,
Your blooms certainly look lovely wrapped around the cover of
my book.
Thank you!

CONTENTS

Title Page

Copyright

Dedication

Chapter 1: An Introduction   1

The History of Dahlias   2

Types of Dahlias   6

Chapter 2: Planning Your Dahlia Garden   11

Choosing the Right Location   12

Preparing the Soil   14

Planting and Growing   18

Companion Planting with Dahlias   21

Chapter 3: Caring for your dahlias   27

Watering and Fertilizing Dahlias   28

Controlling Pests and Diseases   33

Pests: 38

Diseases: 41

Dahlia Growth Problems   43

Staking and Supporting Dahlias   47

Deadheading and Pruning Dahlias   52

Chapter 4: Dahlia Propagation   55

Starting Dahlias from Seed   56

Dividing Dahlias   59

Taking Dahlia Cuttings   64

Chapter 5: Dahlia Preservation   69

Overwintering Dahlias   70

Dahlia Display and Arrangements   74

Capter 6: Resources   79

Dahlia Resources and References   80

CHAPTER 1: AN INTRODUCTION

THE HISTORY OF DAHLIAS

Dahlias are a beautiful and popular flower that can be found in many gardens worldwide. However, many people do not know the interesting history behind this flower.

Dahlias were first discovered in Mexico in the 16th century by the Spanish conquistadors. However, the indigenous people of Mexico were already growing dahlias as a food source, as the tubers were nutritious and tasty.

The Spanish were impressed by the beauty of the flowers and brought them back to Europe, where they quickly became popular among gardeners.

The first dahlia to be scientifically described was Dahlia pinnata, which was named after the Swedish botanist Anders Dahl. The family name, Asteraceae, was given to dahlias in the 19th century, and today they are known as members of the Aster family.

During the 19th century, dahlias became increasingly popular in Europe, and many new varieties were developed. This was also the time when dahlias were introduced to North America. They quickly became a favorite of gardeners in the United States and Canada, where they are still widely grown today.

Today, there are over 40 species of dahlias and thousands of cultivars, each with its unique color, shape, and size. Dahlias come in many different forms, including single, double, cactus, pompon, and decorative varieties.

Dahlias are an integral part of many gardens worldwide, and their popularity shows no signs of waning. They are grown for their beauty, versatility, and ease of cultivation. Whether you are a novice gardener or an experienced horticulturist, dahlias are a great addition to any garden.

TYPES OF DAHLIAS

Dahlias are easy to grow and can be enjoyed in the garden or as cut flowers. There are various types of dahlias available, and each one has its own unique characteristics. The following describes the different categories of dahlias:

Decorative dahlias are the largest of all dahlias and have fully double blooms. They come in a range of colors and can be up to 10 inches in diameter. Decorative dahlias are perfect for cut flowers as they last long and are perfect for arrangements.

Cactus dahlias have spiky petals that curl back towards the stem. They come in a range of colors and can be up to 8 inches in diameter. Cactus dahlias are perfect for adding texture to a garden and are also great for cut flowers.

Anemone dahlias have a central, pom-pom-like disk surrounded by a ring of flat petals. They come in a range of colors and can be up to 5 inches in diameter. Anemone dahlias are perfect for adding a touch of elegance to a garden.

Pompom dahlias have small, ball-shaped blooms that are up to 2 inches in diameter. They come in a range of colors and are perfect for adding a pop of color to a garden.

Waterlily dahlias have double blooms that resemble waterlilies. They come in a range of colors and can be up to 8 inches in diameter. Waterlily dahlias are perfect for adding a touch of whimsy to a garden.

Collarette dahlias have single or double blooms with a ring of smaller petals around the center. They come in a range of colors and are perfect for attracting pollinators to a garden.

Whether you're looking for a large, showy bloom or a smaller, delicate flower, there's a dahlia variety to suit your needs. By understanding the different types of dahlias, you can choose the perfect variety for your garden and enjoy their beauty all season long.

CHAPTER 2: PLANNING

YOUR DAHLIA GARDEN

CHOOSING THE RIGHT LOCATION

When it comes to growing dahlias, one of the most important factors to consider is the location where you will plant them. Choosing the right location can make all the difference in the success of your dahlias.

Dahlias prefer a spot that receives full sunlight for at least six hours a day. They also need a well-draining soil to prevent waterlogging, and prefer an area where there is some protection from the wind.

Keeping these factors in mind when choosing the location, you'll be giving you dahlias the best chance to thrive.

PREPARING THE SOIL

Soil preparation is a crucial step that should not be overlooked. A well-prepared soil will provide your dahlias with the necessary nutrients, moisture, and drainage they need to thrive. Here are some tips for preparing the soil for your dahlias:

Now, prior to preparing the soil, remove any weeds, rocks, or debris from the planting area. This will ensure that your dahlias have enough space to grow and won't have to compete with other plants for nutrients.

It's also a good idea to test your soil's pH level before planting your dahlias. Dahlias prefer a slightly acidic soil with a pH level of 6.0-7.0. You can purchase a soil testing kit from your local garden center or online.

Adding some organic matter to the soil will help improve its structure, fertility, and moisture retention. Compost, aged manure, or leaf mold are excellent sources of organic matter. Simply Mix in a generous amount of organic matter into the soil before planting your dahlias.

As dahlias are heavy feeders and require regular fertilization to grow and bloom, before planting your dahlias, add a slow-release fertilizer to the soil. You can also apply a liquid fertilizer every two to four weeks during the growing season.

Also, if your soil has poor drainage, you can improve it by adding sand or perlite to the soil. This will help prevent waterlogging and root rot. Therefore, preparing the soil is an essential step in growing healthy and beautiful dahlias. By following these tips, you can ensure that your dahlias have the best possible start in life and will reward you with stunning blooms.

PLANTING AND GROWING

Dahlias are usually planted from tubers, which are similar to bulbs. Plant the tubers in the soil with the "eyes" facing up, about six inches deep and one to two feet apart, depending on the variety.

After planting, water the tubers thoroughly to help them settle into the soil. Water regularly, keeping the soil moist but not waterlogged.

Dahlias benefit from regular fertilization throughout the growing season **and I'll cover this in more detail ahead.**

Dahlias can grow quite tall and may require support to keep them from falling over. Use stakes or cages to provide support as the plants grow.

To encourage more blooms, deadhead spent flowers regularly. Also, prune back the plants in late summer or early fall to encourage new growth and more blooms.

By following these steps, you can successfully grow dahlias in your garden.

With their vibrant colors and easy-growing nature, dahlias are a great choice for novice gardeners looking to add some beauty to their outdoor space.

COMPANION PLANTING WITH DAHLIAS

Companion planting is the practice of growing different plants together to maximize their benefits and minimize their drawbacks. It is an ancient technique that has been used for centuries to improve crop yields, control pests, and enhance soil fertility. Dahlias are no exception when it comes to companion planting. Here are some plants that can be grown alongside dahlias to enhance their growth and beauty:

Marigolds are great companion plants for dahlias as they repel harmful insects like aphids, whiteflies, and nematodes. They also attract beneficial insects like ladybugs and lacewings that prey on aphids and other pests. Marigolds are easy to grow and come in a variety of colors that complement dahlias.

Nasturtiums are another great companion plant for dahlias. They have a strong scent that repels pests like aphids, whiteflies, and cucumber beetles. They also attract beneficial insects like bees, butterflies, and hoverflies that help pollinate dahlias. Nasturtiums come in a range of colors that complement dahlias.

Salvia is a great companion plant for dahlias as it attracts hummingbirds and butterflies that help pollinate dahlias. Salvia also has a strong scent that repels pests like deer, rabbits, and squirrels. Salvia comes in a range of colors that complement dahlias.

Cosmos are great companion plants for dahlias as they attract beneficial insects like bees and butterflies that help pollinate dahlias. They also have a strong scent that repels pests like aphids, whiteflies, and cabbage worms. Cosmos come in a range of colors that complement dahlias.

Lavender is a great companion plant for dahlias as it attracts beneficial insects like bees and butterflies that help pollinate dahlias. It also has a strong scent that repels pests like mosquitoes and moths. Lavender comes in a range of colors that complement dahlias.

When planting companion plants with dahlias, it is important to consider their growing requirements. Dahlias prefer well-drained soil and full sun, so make sure to choose companion plants that have similar growing requirements. Also, avoid planting companion plants that are known to be aggressive or invasive as they may compete with dahlias for resources.

In summary, companion planting with dahlias is a great way to enhance their growth and beauty while also repelling pests and attracting beneficial insects. By planting marigolds, nasturtiums, salvia, cosmos, and lavender alongside dahlias, novice gardeners can create a beautiful and healthy garden that is both functional and aesthetically pleasing.

CHAPTER 3: CARING FOR

YOUR DAHLIAS

WATERING AND FERTILIZING DAHLIAS

Watering and fertilizing dahlias are two of the most important aspects of growing these beautiful flowers. Proper watering and fertilizing will ensure that your dahlias grow healthy and strong, producing vibrant blooms that will add color and beauty to your garden.

When it comes to watering your dahlias, it's important to keep in mind that these plants require a lot of water. In fact, they require more water than most other types of flowers.

You should aim to water your dahlias at least once a week, and more often during hot and dry weather. To make sure your dahlias are getting enough water, you can check the soil moisture level by sticking your finger into the soil. If the soil feels dry, it's time to water.

When watering your dahlias, it's important to water deeply to encourage the roots to grow deep into the soil. This will help your dahlias to become more drought-resistant and better able to handle periods of dry weather.

You can also water your dahlias from above or below, depending on your preference. If you water from above, make sure to do it early in the morning or late in the evening to avoid watering during the hottest part of the day.

Fertilizing your dahlias is also important for their growth and health. Dahlias require a lot of nutrients to produce their vibrant blooms, so it's important to feed them regularly. You can use a balanced fertilizer, such as a 10-10-10 or 20-20-20, every two to three weeks during the growing season. You can also use organic fertilizers, such as compost or manure, to add nutrients to the soil.

When fertilizing your dahlias, it's important to follow the instructions on the fertilizer package carefully. Over-fertilizing can cause your dahlias to become too lush and green, which can lead to fewer blooms. Under-fertilizing can also result in poor growth and fewer blooms, so it's important to find the right balance.

In summary, watering and fertilizing your dahlias are two crucial aspects of growing these beautiful flowers. By providing them with enough water and nutrients, you can ensure that your dahlias grow healthy and strong, producing vibrant blooms that will add color and beauty to your garden.

CONTROLLING PESTS AND DISEASES

One of the biggest challenges facing any gardener is the management of pests and diseases. Dahlias are no exception to this rule, and in fact, they can be particularly susceptible to certain issues. Fortunately, there are steps you can take to keep your dahlias healthy and thriving.

The first step in pest and disease control is prevention. One of the best ways to prevent problems is to start with healthy plants. When selecting dahlias for your garden, look for plants that are free of damage or signs of disease. If you're purchasing tubers, make sure they're firm and free of soft spots or mold.

Another key to prevention is good hygiene. Keep your garden clean and tidy, and remove any dead or diseased plant material promptly. This will help prevent the spread of disease and discourage pests from taking up residence in your garden.

Regular inspections are also important. Check your dahlias for signs of pests or disease on a regular basis, and take action if you notice any issues. Early intervention can often prevent problems from becoming more serious.

If you do encounter pests or disease, there are a number of options for treatment. For pests, you might consider using an insecticidal soap or neem oil. For diseases, copper fungicides can be effective, as can sulfur-based treatments. It's important to remember, however, that these treatments should be used judiciously. Overuse of pesticides can harm beneficial insects and upset the delicate balance of your garden ecosystem. Whenever possible, opt for natural solutions and rely on prevention as your first line of defense.

One of the most common problems with dahlias is fungal diseases. These can manifest in a variety of ways, including black spots on the leaves, brown patches on the stems, and wilting or yellowing of the foliage. To prevent fungal diseases, it is important to keep your dahlias well-watered and to avoid getting the leaves wet when watering. You can also use a fungicide spray to protect your plants from these diseases.

Like any plant, dahlias are susceptible to all sorts of pests and diseases. So let's focus on some of the most common pests and diseases that affect dahlias, and what you can do to prevent them and treat them.

PESTS:

Aphids: These tiny insects are a common pest for dahlias and can be found on the leaves and stems of your plants. They suck the sap from the plant, causing the leaves to curl and turn yellow. To prevent aphids, spray your plants with a strong stream of water every couple of days. You can also use insecticidal soap or neem oil to kill them.

Slugs and snails: These pests love to eat the leaves of dahlias, leaving behind large holes and damage. To prevent slugs and snails, try placing a copper strip around the base of your plants. You can also use beer traps or slug pellets to kill them.

Spider mites: These tiny pests are difficult to see with the naked eye, but they can cause serious damage to your plants. They thrive in hot, dry weather and can be prevented with regular watering and misting of your plants. You can also use insecticidal soap or neem oil to kill them.

DISEASES:

Powdery mildew: This fungal disease appears as a white powdery substance on the leaves of your plants. It can be prevented by ensuring good air circulation around your plants, as well as regular watering and fertilizing. If you notice powdery mildew on your plants, try spraying them with a solution of baking soda and water.

Root rot: This disease is caused by overwatering and poor drainage. To prevent root rot, make sure your soil is well-draining and not too moist, and avoid overwatering your plants. If you notice signs of root rot, try removing the affected plants and replanting in fresh soil.

By taking these steps to control pests and diseases, you can keep your dahlias healthy and vibrant. With a little care and attention, you'll be rewarded with a beautiful garden full of thriving plants.

DAHLIA GROWTH PROBLEMS

Dahlias are a beautiful addition to any garden, but they can be challenging for beginners to grow. One of the most common issues that novice gardeners face when growing dahlias is growth problems. In this section, we will discuss the most common growth problems that dahlias face and how to overcome them.

One of the most common growth problems that dahlias face is **stunted**

growth. This can be caused by several factors, including poor soil quality, lack of nutrients, and overwatering. To overcome this problem, it is important to ensure that your dahlias are planted in well-draining soil and that they receive the nutrients they need. You can add compost or organic fertilizer to the soil to improve its quality.

Another common growth problem that dahlias face is **yellowing leaves**. This can be caused by several factors, including nutrient deficiencies, pests, and disease. To overcome this problem, it is important to inspect your dahlias regularly for signs of pests or disease. If you notice any issues, take action immediately to prevent them from spreading. Additionally, make sure that your dahlias are receiving the nutrients they need like nitrogen and magnesium, by fertilizing them regularly.

Wilting flowers are another common growth problem that dahlias face. This can be caused by a lack of water, overwatering, or disease. To overcome this problem, make sure that your dahlias are receiving the right amount of water. Water them deeply once a week, and make sure that the soil is well-draining. Additionally, make sure to inspect your dahlias regularly for signs of disease, and take action immediately if you notice any issues.

Finally, while dahlias are generally easy to grow, although they can be prone to certain problems that can affect their health and beauty. By being aware of these issues and taking steps to prevent them, you can ensure that your dahlias thrive and provide you with beautiful blooms year after year.

STAKING AND SUPPORTING DAHLIAS

Dahlias are beautiful and vibrant flowers that can add a touch of elegance and color to any garden. However, as they grow, they can become top-heavy and may require staking and support to keep them from falling over. This is especially true for larger varieties of dahlias, which can grow up to six feet tall.

The first step in staking your dahlias

is to choose the right stakes. Bamboo and metal stakes are popular choices, but wooden stakes can also work. Make sure the stakes are tall enough to support the height of your dahlias.

It's best to stake your dahlias early in the growing season, before they become too tall and top-heavy. This will help prevent damage to the stems and flowers when you insert the stakes.

Once you have your stakes in place, tie the stems of your dahlias to the stakes using soft twine or plant ties. Be careful not to tie the stems too tightly, as this can damage the plant. Leave some room for the stems to grow and expand.

If you have a large dahlia plant with multiple stems, a support ring can be an effective way to keep it upright. A support ring is a metal or plastic ring that you place around the plant, and then tie the stems to the ring.

If your dahlias are still leaning or falling over, you can provide additional support by using a plant support netting or a trellis. These can be placed around the plant and provide additional support for the stems.

Staking and supporting your dahlias is essential for ensuring their health and beauty. With the right stakes and support, your dahlias will stand tall and proud, adding a touch of elegance to your garden.

In summary, growing dahlias can be challenging for novice gardeners, but with the right knowledge and care, you can overcome any growth problems that your dahlias may face. By ensuring that your dahlias are planted in a sunny position, in well-draining soil, receiving the nutrients they need, and being inspected regularly for signs of pests or disease, you can enjoy a beautiful and healthy dahlia garden.

DEADHEADING AND PRUNING DAHLIAS

Deadheading and pruning are important tasks in the care and maintenance of dahlias. Deadheading is the process of removing spent flowers from the plant, while pruning involves cutting back the plant to promote new growth. These tasks are essential to ensure that your dahlias bloom continuously and remain healthy throughout the growing season.

Deadheading dahlias is a simple but crucial task that can be done by hand. Simply pinch off the dead flowers at the base of the stem, just above the first set of leaves. This will encourage the plant to produce more flowers and prevent it from using up energy to produce seeds. Deadheading should be done regularly, at least once a week, throughout the growing season.

Pruning dahlias is another important task that can be done to maintain the shape and size of the plant. Pruning should be done in early summer when the plants have reached a height of 12 to 18 inches. To prune, use a sharp pair of scissors or pruning shears and cut back the plant to just above a set of leaves. This will encourage the plant to branch out and produce more flowers.

In summary, deadheading and pruning are essential tasks in the care and maintenance of dahlias. These tasks will ensure that your dahlias bloom continuously and remain healthy throughout the growing season.

CHAPTER 4: DAHLIA PROPAGATION

STARTING DAHLIAS FROM SEED

While many gardeners choose to propagate dahlias from tubers, starting dahlias from seed can be a fun and rewarding experience for the novice gardener.

Dahlias are warm-season plants that thrive in full sun. They can be started from seed indoors in late winter or early spring, or sown directly into the ground after the last frost date. If you choose to start your dahlias indoors, be sure to provide them with plenty of light and warmth until they are ready to be transplanted.

To start dahlias from seed, fill a seed tray with seed-starting mix. Press the seeds lightly into the soil, making sure that they are covered with a thin layer of soil. Water the seeds gently and place the tray in a warm, sunny location. Keep the soil moist but not waterlogged.

Once the seedlings are large enough to handle, transplant them into individual pots or containers. Be sure to keep the soil moist and provide them with plenty of light and warmth. Once the danger of frost has passed, transplant your dahlias into the garden.

In your pre-prepared soil, dig a hole that is large enough to accommodate the root ball of the dahlia seedling and fill it with soil. Water the soil well to ensure that it is moist but not waterlogged.

DIVIDING DAHLIAS

Dahlias are a popular choice for gardeners because of their vibrant colors and stunning blooms. However, to keep your dahlias blooming year after year, it is essential to divide them regularly.

Dividing dahlias is a simple process that can be done in the spring or fall,and ensures that your plant remains healthy and productive

Dahlias are perennials, which means

they grow back each year from the same root system. However, over time, the roots can become crowded, which can cause the plant to produce fewer flowers or even stop blooming altogether. Dividing dahlias is an effective way to prevent this from happening.

When you divide a dahlia, you separate the plant into smaller sections, each with its own root system. This allows the plant to grow more vigorously and produce more blooms.

The best time to divide dahlias is either in the spring or fall. Spring division is best if you live in a colder climate since it gives the plant more time to establish its roots before winter. Fall division is ideal if you live in a warmer climate since the ground is still warm, and the plant has time to establish its roots before the cold weather sets in.

Dividing dahlias is a straightforward process. Begin by digging up the entire plant, being careful not to damage the roots. Once the plant is out of the ground, gently shake off any excess soil and remove any dead or diseased sections. Use a sharp, clean knife or garden shears to cut the plant into smaller sections, making sure that each section has at least one healthy stem and a portion of the root system.

After dividing the plant, replant each section in a new location or container with fresh soil. Make sure to water the plants thoroughly and keep them well-watered until they establish themselves in their new location.

Dividing dahlias is a simple process that can help keep your plants healthy and productive. By dividing your dahlias every few years, you can ensure that you get the most blooms possible from your plants. So, if you're a novice gardener looking to grow beautiful dahlias, don't forget to divide them regularly. Your plants will thank you for it!

TAKING DAHLIA CUTTINGS

Taking cuttings from dahlias is an essential task when it comes to propagating new plants. It is an easy and cost-effective method to increase your collection and share your favorite cultivars with friends and family. In this section, we will guide you through the process of taking dahlia cuttings, from selecting a suitable mother plant to rooting and potting your cuttings.

The first step in taking dahlia cuttings is to select a healthy mother plant. Look for a plant that is vigorous, disease-free, and has plenty of stems to choose from.

Choose a stem that is about 3-4 inches long, with at least two pairs of leaves and a growing tip. Avoid selecting stems that are too woody or too soft, as they are less likely to root successfully.

Using a sharp and clean pair of scissors or pruners, make a clean cut just below a node (the point where a leaf attaches to the stem) at a 45-degree angle. Remove the lower pair of leaves, leaving only the top pair intact. This will reduce the amount of moisture lost through transpiration and help the cutting to focus its energy on root development.

To root the cutting, fill a small pot with a well-draining potting mix, such as a mixture of peat moss and perlite. Make a hole in the soil with a pencil or your finger, and insert the cutting into the hole. Firm the soil around the cutting to ensure good soil-to-stem contact. Water the cutting thoroughly, and place it in a warm, bright spot, away from direct sunlight.

After a few weeks, you should start to see new growth emerging from the cutting. Once the roots have developed and the cutting has become established, you can pot it up into a larger container or transplant it into your garden.

When potting up your cutting, use a well-draining soil mix and a pot that is slightly larger than the root ball. Water the plant thoroughly, and place it in a sunny spot, where it will receive at least 6 hours of sunlight per day.

In summary, taking dahlia cuttings is a simple and rewarding way to propagate new plants. With a little bit of patience and care, you can create a beautiful collection of dahlias that will bring joy to your garden for years to come.

CHAPTER 5: DAHLIA PRESERVATION

OVERWINTERING DAHLIAS

Dahlias are a beautiful addition to any garden, but they require some special care during the winter months. Overwintering dahlias is an essential part of maintaining healthy plants that will bloom year after year. Here are some tips and tricks for novices on how to overwinter dahlias.

First, it's important to understand that dahlias are not frost-hardy. This means that they will not survive in freezing temperatures. Before the first frost, you must dig up the dahlia tubers and store them indoors. The ideal time to do this is after the foliage has died back but before the ground has frozen. This is usually around mid to late October in most areas.

To dig up the dahlias, use a garden fork to loosen the soil around the plant. Then, carefully lift the tubers out of the ground, being sure not to damage them. Gently shake off any excess soil and trim the stems down to a few inches. Do not wash the tubers, as this can increase the risk of mold and rot.

Next, you need to store the dahlias in a cool, dry place. A basement or garage is an ideal location. You can also use a cardboard box, a paper bag, or a plastic container with ventilation holes.

Fill the container with peat moss, sawdust, or vermiculite to keep the tubers dry. Be sure to label the container with the dahlia variety and the date of storage.

Check on the dahlias periodically throughout the winter to ensure that they are not drying out or becoming too damp. If they are too dry, mist them with water. If they are too damp, remove them from the container and allow them to air out for a few hours before returning them to storage.

In the spring, you can plant the dahlias again after the danger of frost has passed. Simply dig a hole and place the tuber in it, covering it with soil. Water the plant well and wait for it to sprout. With these tips and tricks, you can successfully overwinter dahlias and enjoy beautiful blooms year after year.

DAHLIA DISPLAY AND ARRANGEMENTS

As a novice gardener, one of the most exciting things about growing dahlias is being able to display their stunning blooms. Dahlias are known for their wide range of colors, shapes, and sizes, making them a versatile flower for a variety of occasions. Here are some tips and tricks for creating beautiful dahlia displays and arrangements.

First, it's important to choose the

right vase or container for your dahlias. Tall, slender vases work well for long-stemmed dahlias, while shorter, wider vases are better suited for smaller, bushier blooms. Make sure to clean your vase thoroughly before use to prevent any bacteria from infecting your flowers.

When arranging your dahlias, consider using a variety of colors and sizes to create a dynamic, eye-catching display. Place larger blooms in the center of your arrangement and surround them with smaller blooms. If you're using dahlias with different stem lengths, trim them to the same length so they sit evenly in your vase.

Another popular way to display dahlias is in a bouquet. To create a beautiful dahlia bouquet, start by selecting a few larger blooms as the focal point. Add in some smaller dahlias, greenery, and filler flowers such as baby's breath or ferns to create texture and depth. Tie the stems together with ribbon or twine, and trim them to the desired length.

If you're looking for a more unique way to display your dahlias, consider using them in a wreath or centerpiece. For a dahlia wreath, start with a wire or foam wreath form and attach dahlias using floral wire. You can also add in greenery or other flowers to create a fuller look. For a dahlia centerpiece, fill a shallow bowl or basket with oasis foam and arrange dahlias and other flowers as desired.

No matter how you choose to display your dahlias, make sure to keep them hydrated by changing the water every few days.

Ensure you remove any leaves that will be submerged in the water to prevent bacteria growth.

With these tips and tricks, you'll be able to create beautiful dahlia displays and arrangements that will brighten up any room.

CAPTER 6: RESOURCES

DAHLIA RESOURCES AND REFERENCES

As a novice gardener, it's important to have access to reliable resources and references when it comes to growing dahlias. Fortunately, there are many resources available to help you learn more about these beautiful flowers and how to cultivate them successfully.

One excellent resource for dahlia growers is the American Dahlia Society (ADS). This organization offers a wealth of information on all aspects of dahlia growing, including tips for planting, fertilizing, watering, and pest control. The ADS also sponsors dahlia shows and competitions, which can be a great way to connect with other dahlia enthusiasts and learn from experienced growers.

Another great resource for dahlia information is the National Garden Bureau (NGB). This organization provides a variety of resources for home gardeners, including detailed growing guides, plant profiles, and gardening tips. The NGB also sponsors a "Year of" program each year, which focuses on a specific type of plant (including dahlias in 2019), and provides a wealth of information on that plant throughout the year.

If you're looking for more in-depth information on dahlia cultivation, there are many books available on the subject. Some excellent titles to consider include "The Dahlia Primer" by Arthur O. Tucker and Margaret G. Smith, and "The Plant Lover's Guide to Dahlias" by Andy Vernon. These books offer detailed information on everything from selecting the right varieties for your garden to caring for your plants throughout the growing season.

In addition to these resources, there are many online forums and social media groups dedicated to dahlia cultivation. These can be a great way to connect with other dahlia growers, ask questions, share tips and tricks, and stay up-to-date on the latest trends and best practices in dahlia cultivation.

Whether you're a seasoned gardener or a complete novice, there are many resources available to help you grow beautiful dahlias in your own garden. By taking advantage of these resources and references, you can learn everything you need to know to cultivate these stunning flowers and enjoy their beauty year after year.

Made in the USA
Monee, IL
07 September 2023

dc1b76e4-05aa-4310-b878-d29c056d19b2R01